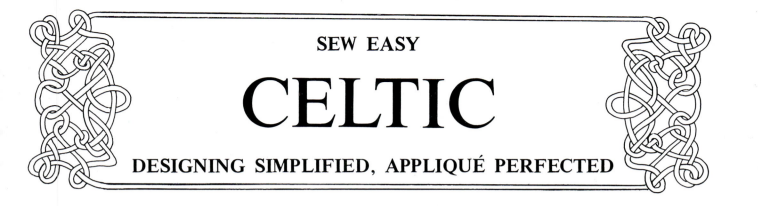

SEW EASY
CELTIC
DESIGNING SIMPLIFIED, APPLIQUÉ PERFECTED

By

ANGELA MADDEN

i

Acknowledgments :

Very grateful thanks are due to the following . . . . . .

My family, Denis, Laura and Rob for coping with my 'Celtomania'.

"Peartree Quilters", fellow quilters, advisers and long standing friends, Nora Field, Chris Graves, Muriel Gent, Diana Howes, Dorothy Holman, Sara Hibbert, Rita Hodges, Alison King, Kathleen McMahon and especially Jane Plowman for proof reading.

"The Maddening Crowd Quilters" (their choice of name!) Jean Brown, Adrienne Cave, June Cowin, Theresa Doolan, Linda Gahagan, Christine Kent, Kate and Judy Wilson and Mandy Smith, for co-operating with my experiments.

Special thanks to Alan Smith and Nuri Wyeth for their assistance . . . . and to numerous quilting colleagues for their support and encouragement.

Credits:

Book design, photography and illustrations . . . . Angela Madden
Celtic background information . . . . Eileen Daly
Back cover portrait photography . . . . Mary Daly
Editor . . . . Theresa Wonnet

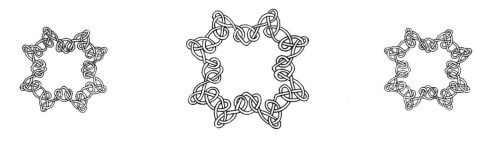

M.C.Q. Publications
19 Barlings Road
Harpenden, Herts AL5 2AL
England

Sew Easy Celtic 1993 by Angela Madden
ISBN 0 9521060 0 0
First Edition 1993

Contents

Introduction

"Long, long ago, beyond the misty space
Of twice a thousand years,
In Erin old there lived a mighty race
Taller than Roman spears . . . . "

'The Celts' . . . . Thomas D'Arcy McGee 1825—68

This romantic notion of the Celts is widespread today, associating them almost exclusively with Scotland, Ireland, Wales, The Isle of Man and Cornwall. In reality the origin of the people described is much broader, and they would not have recognised a common identity or name. The Ancient Greeks spoke of the 'Keltoi', meaning 'barbarians', but never applied this title to the British Isles. The Romans called the people there 'Picts', a descriptive name for their love of colour, skill with enamelling on metal and fondness for painting their naked bodies with patterned symbols and charms, for battle. The idea of a 'Celtic' culture, emerged over one hundred years ago, conceived by historians, who recognised linking traits in archaeological finds throughout Europe.

'Celtic' Society emerged around 500—450 B.C. in Central Europe. The discovery of Iron enabled tribal groups to flourish and spread from their origin near the Alps to the continents' far fringes and into Asia. They invaded Delphi and conquered the Infant Rome. Family groupings, under the rule and protection of Kings, farmed, traded, engaged in sports, made music and fine metalwork, as well as being ferocious warriors. Having no written language, tradition, history and law were verbally handed down by their priests, the Druids. We know little today of their beliefs.

The rise and expansion of the Roman Empire and the spread of Christianity in 5th Century overtook the Celts. Their influence faded to the more remote areas unreached by the Romans. One such area was South West Ireland, the site of my own family roots in County Kerry. The first Celtic writing (called 'Ogham') is thought to have developed there, and it is also the location of many tales from Celtic mythology. Two thousand year old stone dwellings and Celtic ring forts still exist, and the Gaelic language spoken there has direct links with those ancient times.

Celtic Knotwork, with complicated interlaced cord patterns is thought to be Asiatic in origin, reaching Ireland via Germany. Christianity first condemned this art style as atheistic. It was not representational, having developed from the belief that to reproduce the works of God was forbidden. Later monastery manuscript art adopted Interlace and developed it to a peak in 8th Century with The Book of Kells now held at Trinity College, Dublin. Centuries later the Victorians also loved the style, leaving numerous war memorials, jewellery etc so decorated.

The ancient scribes had a good knowledge of geometry, and were technically expert in its execution. Unfortunately like so many people I do not share those skills. This book results partly from a search to find an alternative method to design interlaced patterns easily and swiftly, and partly from my love of the unspoilt Kerry scenery and the 'imaginings' it stirs of long gone peoples, who left their distinctive mark on European history. It is my hope that by sharing my methods and favourite places with you, my enthusiasm might encourage you to try this very pleasantly addictive artform.

Angela Madden

Designing a Celtic Style Medallion

Welcome to Celtic design, or perhaps it should be 'Céad Míle Fáilte'. It is much easier than you would ever imagine. There are no complicated geometric techniques or calculations in this system. No previous artistic expertise is necessary. Celtic designing can be absorbing and fun, with a built in element of unpredictability which adds surprise and excitement.

Tools for Designing

1. Tracing paper
2. Ruler
3. Pencil
4. Black felt tipped pen
5. Soft eraser
6. Scrap paper
7. Scissors

Tip

Greaseproof paper is a very efficient and cheap substitute for tracing paper. (Unfortunately it is not available in U.S.A. and wax paper which might be considered the nearest equivalent is unsuitable.)

Begin by creating a medallion design suitable for a cushion front or quilt block.

1. On scrap paper . . . . draw a 6in. square. This represents ¼ of the finished design. It will therefore produce a 12in. completed medallion.

2. Mark the corners of the square A. B. C. D. in the order illustrated.

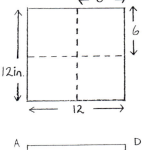

3. Link corners B & D with a diagonal line. This creates two triangles E & F.

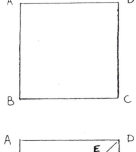

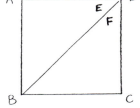

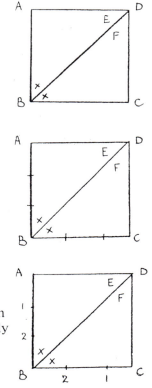

4. In corner B mark each side of the diagonal line clearly with an 'X'. This will be the centre of the completed design.

5. Divide sides A B and B C into 1/3 portions as illustrated. These form registration points for linking sections together.

6. Number both registration points on each line identically Place both number 2's near to corner B.

That's as Geometric as it gets Folks!

Design Lines

Set your 6in. square aside for a few minutes, while we consider some practical design hints.

Celtic interlaced designs fool the eye into thinking they are made from cords. These weave over and under each other, and often display neither beginning nor end, but are continuous throughout the pattern.

With design experience any number of cords can be interlaced, creating large and complex designs. The underlying principles remain constant. For practice and simplicity we will use two cords. Each will begin as a single, lightly drawn pencil line, representing one side edge of the cord. Once the design is satisfactory, the second side edge will be added.

Definition of both edges of all cords is necessary to enable the finished effect to be clearly seen. It will also clarify at a later stage the correct 'over and under' interlacing of the cords.

Regard this part of the design process as 'doodling'. We have all indulged in this to pass time, so can claim to be 'expert' by now!

Struggling for artistic perfection at this stage is both inhibiting and unnecessary.

RELAX . . . . prepare to 'doodle' . . . . having first read the following tips . . . . .

Be on the lookout for . . . .

1. **'Wiggly' lines** : remember that the lines you draw will represent cords coiling around each other. They should form flowing rounded curves, not wiggles and zig-zags. (However the odd deviation caused by a shaky hand is unavoidable.)

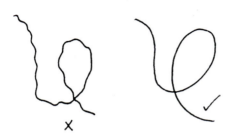

2. **'Shrunken Loops'** : small loops are more difficult to appliqué. Aim to make all loops into 'plump teardrops'.

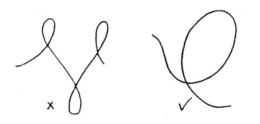

3. **'Lonely Loops'** : these are loops which stand alone and are not interwoven into the design by another cord. The occasional one is fine, especially at the corners of a medallion. If several are present, the interest and complexity of the pattern diminishes. Aim to thread all loops on another cord.

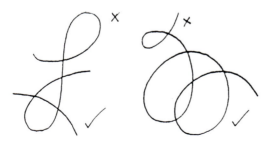

RULE TO REMEMBER
Each line may only cross one other at any crossing point in the design. The nearer this cross is to a right angle the clearer the crossing will be.

4. **'Confused Crossings'** : remember that you are aiming for clear interlaced designs. Each cord should be easy to follow and not get mixed up in a 'tangle'.

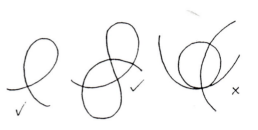

5. **'Cramped Spaces'** : allow space between cords, to allow the addition of the second line with ease. Crossing lines must never run along on top of each other.

DRAWING DESIGN LINES

Returning to your 6in. square and using pencil, very lightly until confident, draw your first design line as follows. (These instructions will enable you to design your own unique medallion. Alternatively copy my examples until you gain confidence.)

1. Starting on line A B registration point 1, doodle a simple curving and looping line through triangle E to any point on the diagonal line.

2. Continue through triangle F roughly reversing the design and ending on registration point 1 on line B C.

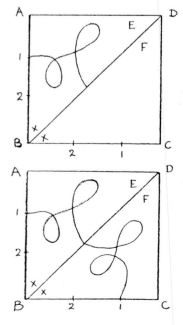

DO NOT WORRY, if the designs in both triangles are not absolutely exact mirror images of each other. It could even work to your advantage later on.

3. To add the 2nd design line, begin on line A B registration point 2, and doodle to the diagonal as before, interacting with the previous line as you wish. Roughly reverse the design in triangle F as before. End on registration point 2 on line B C.

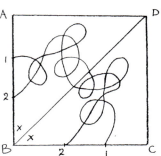

4. Check back to the 'Be on the lookout for . . .' tips previously given. Alter your design if necessary.

POINT OF INTEREST : the doodles in my diagrams will produce the following design. (All examples given in this Section produce designs which are extra to the 16 full sized ones given later.)

DO NOT . . . attempt to complete your design at this stage. Even if you have copied my example your design will look different and therefore unique, as the size of loops and spaces, and variations in their positions can help create endless alternative effects. Add or subtract a loop, curve or straighten a line and designs alter Kaliedoscope fashion. Many patterns do not look 'promising' at this stage . . . . 'hang in there' and 'have faith', you will soon be pleasantly surprised . . . . maybe even amazed!

ADDING DOUBLE OUTLINES . . . . CREATING CORDS

Each line in your drawing needs another approximately ¼ in. away from it, and parallel throughout, to create the impression of a solid cord. Always add this in pencil, but not yet.

POINTS TO NOTE :

1. We are ignoring all 'over' and 'under' interlacings for the present.

2. For designs intended to be bias appliquéd, artistic perfection is unnecessary when adding double lines. Time spent in this pursuit is time wasted.

3. Although I am chiefly concerned with designing for appliqué, it is a bonus to realise the suitability of these designs for machine embroidery, or quilting alone. In both these techniques you may wish to follow an exactly drawn design. Perfectly distanced double outlines can easily be achieved by using two pencils taped together. Allow one to follow the original design line whilst the other creates the new one.

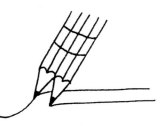

Useful Tip : if a very fine double outline is required, tape 2 diary or 'golf score' pencils together. A cocktail stick and a pencil also works well.

4. Adding double outlines can sometimes highlight spacing problems. For this reason the drawn width of the cord should always be the same as is required in the finished design.

LOOKING AT LOOPS

1. If all the loops in a design face in one direction, the second line creating the cord always travels on the same side of the loops, i.e. outside or inside.

In the previous example it travels on the outside of all loops. Lines which double up on the outside of loops enlarge them. More space is taken up around their perimeter, bringing them nearer to neighbouring cords. If space between cords is tight, this can be a problem.

2. If loops in a design face in opposite directions, the second line is forced to change its position. It moves from the outside of one loop, to the inside of another, depending on which way they face.

Lines which double up on the inside of a loop make them smaller, diminishing the inside space. If loops are drawn small in the first place this can also cause problems and distort the proportions of a design. The solution to both of these problems is . . . .

THE SWITCH . . . .

Think ahead, when double outlining as you approach a new loop. Choose to double up on either the inside, or the outside, by deciding which will most enhance the design. If it is necessary to change sides of the original line, do so on a straight run of cord before you reach the loop.

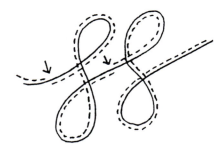

The switch can be easily disguised and the resulting bumps erased.

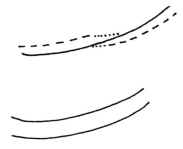

With these guidelines in mind, double outlines can now be pencilled in. Ignore points where lines cross and just draw straight through them as though they didn't exist.

ACHIEVING SYMMETRY

When all the double outlining has been completed, study your 1/4 design carefully to decide which 1/8th you prefer . . . . triangle E or triangle F? Even minor differences can make one section more or less attractive, and the existence of these differences provides you with choice. It will now be necessary to accurately reproduce the chosen triangle to achieve a symmetrical design.

Of course it would be possible to start designing using only an 1/8th section. This would remove the above choice. For the minimum extra effort involved in producing 1/4 design it also enables 1/2 design to be examined if a mirror is held against either side A B or B C.

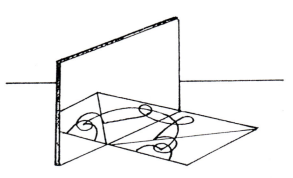

Carefully cut out your chosen triangle, putting the other aside.

DEFINING OUTLINES

Using black felt tipped pen, mark over your pencilled cord outlines. Each time a crossing is reached mark only the boundary lines, leaving the middle blank.

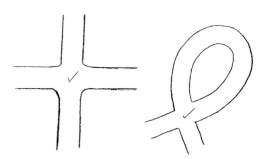

1. Take a sheet of tracing paper which is large enough to accommodate the completed design. (In this case 12in. square minimum . . . I would advise allowing some additional border space.) Fold it in half, creasing the fold very sharply.

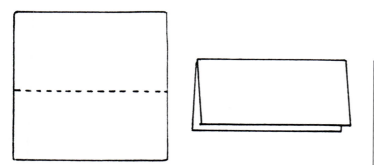

2. Fold in half again in the opposite direction, into quarters. Exactly match and sharply crease the folds.

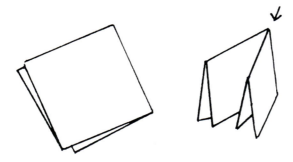

3. Identify the corner at which all the folds meet. This is the centre of the paper and will likewise be the centre of your medallion design.

4. Fold the paper diagonally with the fold once again running through this 'centre' corner.

5. Slip the chosen 1/8th design under one layer of the folded tracing paper into the triangular pocket which the folding has created.

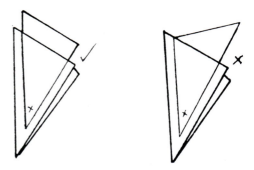

IMPORTANT : check . . . .

(a) That the 'X' marked on corner B goes right down into the folded point of the tracing paper.

(b) That the outer edges of both scrap and tracing paper run parallel to each other. If they do not . . . . remove the 1/8th section, turn the tracing paper over without unfolding it, replacing the 1/8th section in the uppermost triangular pocket as before.

(c) That you can see the double outlines through only one layer of tracing paper.

6. Using felt pen, trace the double outline 1/8th section through the single layer of tracing paper.

7. Remove and set aside 1/8th design.

8. It is now possible to trace the design through to the other side of the fold in the tracing paper. Careful refolding (matching fold lines exactly) will enable each section to be completed by tracing through, until the medallion is whole. It does not matter that some sections are traced on either side of the paper, they are still easily visible.

9. Lay out the completed design and admire your handiwork as a Celtic designer. With 'overs and unders' added it will look GREAT!

It is best to wait until this stage of completion before clarifying which cords go over or under others as they weave around the pattern. It looks possible at an earlier stage. However as sections are reversed during tracing, previously interwoven sections would become mirror immages, and not continuous interlaced Celtic style designs.

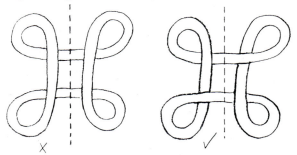

1. Return to using pencil until you are completely certain that the interlaced effect is correct throughout the design. Begin at any random crossing and mark the outer edges of the cord which will cross the intersection on top.

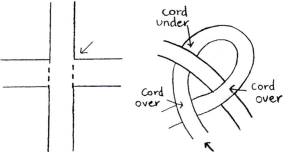

2. Follow one cord at a time around the design, marking its passage alternately over and under all other cords it meets. The end will correctly sequence with the point at which you started. If it does not . . . . retrace your path, and check for mistakes until it does.

3. Do not be tempted to jump from cord to cord marking intersections. It is very easy to 'chase' a mistake around a design, moving it from cord to cord without actually locating it!

4. When one cord has been successfully completed, begin the same process with another. (When using only two cords the interlacing of one will simultaneously interlace the other.) Start anywhere as before, but this time take your cue from an already completed intersection. Check **all** intersections have been interlaced.

USEFUL TIP : draw a light pencil line along the centre of the cord which you are following, as you go. This will keep you on the right course and should the phone or similar divert you, it will be easy to see where to begin on your return.

Should your 'overs and unders' not work out correctly . . . . there is nothing wrong with the design . . . . ONLY THE DESIGNER! Take a break, then check again.

However, should you wish to add in extra cords, or loops on existing cords at this stage, with interlacing already complete, it is not always possible to lace them in correctly. Retrace the whole design without 'overs and unders', add the new elements, and interlace entire design as before.

INCREASING DESIGN POSSIBILITIES . . . .

as confidence grows . . . .

Now that you can create a regularly shaped Celtic style medallion, try one with an irregular shape.

Option 1

1. Draw a square as before and follow instructions 1 to 6 on page 1.

2. Doodle your first design cord from registration point 1 on line A B through triangle E as before ending on any point on the diagonal.

3. Doodle a totally different design path through triangle F to registration point 1 on line B C.

4. Add the second cord design line in exactly the same way, creating an asymmetric 1/4 section, ready to be double outlined, with blank intersections as before.

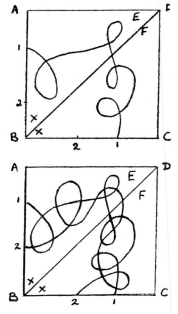

The above 1/4 design will produce both of the following medallions.

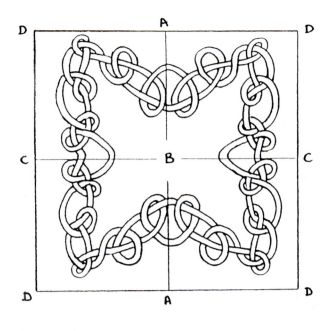

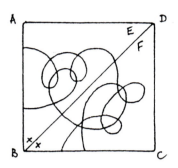

Design A: in which square sides A B and B C meet their mirror image, (except for interlacings) the 1/4 design is placed in the pocket of the folded tracing paper, and the design is completed in the usual way.

Option 2

As per Option 1, with the variation that the registration points on A B and B C are placed at random, and therefore only match with their mirror image.

Random registration points enable medallions with thin 'waists' to be created if cords originate and terminate near corner B along one side.

This 1/4 design produces the following medallion.

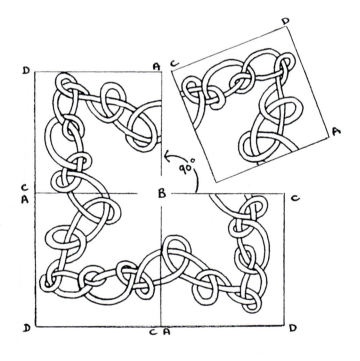

Design B: in which square side A B repeatedly meets side B C the design 1/4 is turned through 90° and traced in turn onto each 1/4 section of the previously folded, but now opened flat, paper. The creased folds help to register the design correctly.

Interlacing is added to the completed designs as before. Both these designs are achievable because registration points on A B and B C enable them to be matched up.

Registration points therefore serve the following purposes . . . .

1. They enable design sections to match.

2. They can control the shape of designs where sections meet.

3. In continuous designs they mark the entry and exit of cords from section to section. In multi-cord designs the number of cords equals the number of registration points, i.e. 6 cords = 6 registration points on both lines A B & B C . . . .

— 7 —

UNLESS . . . . (a) cord loops fall exactly on lines A B and B C in which an extra registration point is created by the top of each such loops.

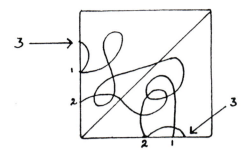

(b) Option 3: it is possible for design lines to double back and exit on the same square side as they started. In this case double the number of registration points are needed on this square side. Such designs, are non-continuous when the full medallion is drawn.

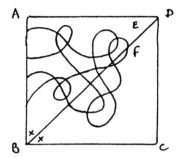

In this example all cords both begin and end on side A B. The design created will therefore be in two separate half sections, as shown from the completed medallion this 1/4 design will produce. (Perhaps a little dull in the centre A B?)

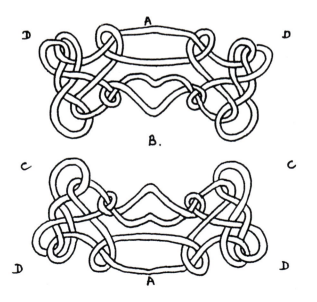

These sectional designs can be combined in a number of ways . . . . so do check the

possibilities of any design before abandoning it as one having little worth.

The previous design has a few alternatives to check . . . .
Cut centrally through the tracing paper separating both designs. Move the bottom section to the top. Overlap the paper edges until the designs come together. They form a new waisted medallion with corner A now positioned at design centre. (Designs can be readily stuck together again with clear tape.) The centre cords can be crossed, uniting both sections, however the interlacing will be incorrect on one side.

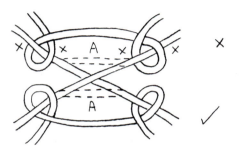

If you like the newly formed medallion it would be worthwhile to re-trace one half and interlace it correctly. Keep the section that would not interlace.

In this example the new medallion would look like this . . . .

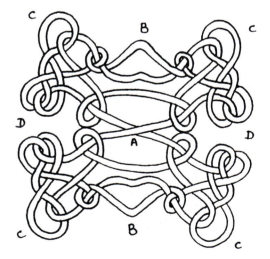

Do not forget to view all irregular medallions 'side on' too. They look very different.

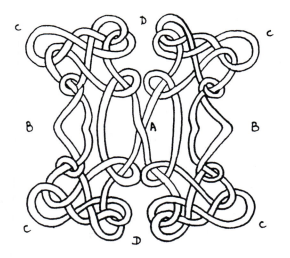

create border designs. Corner loops can be linked together making sections continuous. Again they will interlace correctly. Trace one design repeatedly, turning it upside down at times to vary the effect.

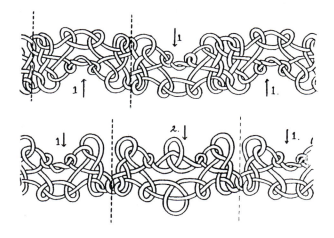

If you particularly wanted a sectional design try eliminating the dull middle part as follows . . . . return to the spare section that would not interlace. This time cut it centrally through the design cords from A to B. Overlap the cut edges bringing the more intricately knotted 'shoulders' of the design closer together.

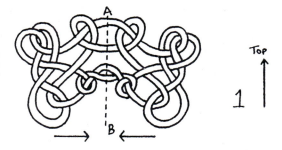

This improves the effect considerably.

Another possibility is to make the middle more interesting, by adding loops.

The extra loops work wonders and will interlace correctly as an even number of 'overs and unders' have been created between existing intersections. Both these new sections can be used individually or alternately to

TRANSFERRING THE DESIGN TO FABRIC

Method 1 : for Quilting or Embroidery

1. Fold the background fabric onto which the design is to be transferred, into quarters and lightly press the folds.

2. Match the fabric folds with the horizontal and vertical paper folds, ensuring that it is correctly centred.

3. With fabric right side uppermost, on top of the design paper place both on one of the following light sources.

(a) A light box.

(b) A bright window.

(c) A glass topped table with a light placed underneath.

This will enable you to see the design clearly through the fabric. It is possible to see through very dark, even black fabric in this way.

4. Trace the double outline of the design onto the fabric using one of the following as appropriate.

(a) **Water erasable pen** . . . . avoid using on coloured fabric, as the chemicals it contains may discolour the cloth, if not completely removed by washing out.

(b) **Light erasable pen** . . . . if you are a speedy worker and will do the sewing before the lines fade. If you do have to interrupt your work, store it in a dark place, in a bag.

(c) **Silver pencil**, suitable for light coloured fabrics.

(d) **Dressmaker's chalk pencil**, suitable for dark fabrics . . . . wears off easily.

(e) **A well sharpened coloured pencil**, used lightly, colour as per fabric.

(f) **A sliver of soap**, suitable for dark fabrics . . . . also wears off easily.

Method 2 : for Bias Appliqué

1. Using an embroidery transfer pencil, (the type which is used on paper and ironed onto fabric) draw a firm line down the centre of each cord on the tracing paper design. This line will be continuous at intersections, on all 'over' cords. It will temporarily discontinue where cords pass underneath.

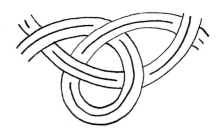

2. Fold, press and match fabric and paper design as per points 1 and 2 in previous method, checking that the right side of the fabric is next to the transfer pencilled side of the paper. Place pins only at the outer edges of the design, clear of the pencil lines. They will hinder ironing if placed on the design itself, or in its centre.

3. Press steadily with a dry iron set at moderate heat, having laid the fabric down with the paper uppermost. This will transfer the design lines to the fabric. Move the iron very slowly over the design to ensure that the heat fully activates the pencil.

4. Check that the transfer is successful by removing one pin at a time and lifting the paper to see underneath, without disturbing its position. If necessary replace the paper and press again. The transferred lines will be covered by the appliqué, but will clearly show which cords pass over or under at any intersection, during construction.

Tools for BIAS APPLIQUÉ & QUILTING

1. Rotary Cutter
2. Rotary Ruler
3. Cutting board
4. Bias Bars . . . . (metal or polyester bars, sold in sets of 3 sizes . . . approx 1/4 in . . . 3/8 in . . . 1/2 in from specialist supplies, see back page.)
5. Transparent nylon thread . . . . 'clear' for light fabrics . . . . 'smoke' for dark.
6. No. 70 or equivalent sewing machine needle.
7. Sewing machine walking foot. (Optional)

Fabric cut into thin strips at 45° to the woven thread has a wonderful capacity to mould itself around curves. Cutting in this way is cutting 'on the bias', and the fabric strips are therefore 'bias strips'.

It is possible to use different types of fabric, but generally agreed that 100% cotton is the easiest to handle. However 'difficult' fabrics e.g. Lurex, become very much easier using this appliqué method. Being cut on the bias ensures such problem fabric will not fray as it would if cut on the straight of the grain.

There is no advantage to be achieved from having long lengths of continuous bias for use in Celtic appliqué. In fact they cause difficulty, joins are unsightly and even quite short lengths e.g. 3 ins. can be used in most designs. The ends of all strips are hidden beneath an 'over' cord, rendering them invisible and creating the illusion of a continuous cord.

The maximum effect is achieved by having clearly contrasting coloured cords on a plain fabric background. The cords can be effectively cut from patterned fabric, plaids and candy stripes are particularly good but need extra attention during cutting as will be explained later. Patterns with strong diagonals which are printed at 45° are best avoided, since they are difficult to cut exactly along the pattern and discrepancies show.

Fabrics should be pre-washed to prevent colour bleeding or shrinkage in future laundering, otherwise dry clean.

Estimating Bias Yardage

It is very difficult to give specific fabric requirements accurately. The same sized Celtic design can vary enormously in both number of cords and complexity of pattern.

Introduce different coloured cords and without seeing the design I'm lost!

However, the following suggestions can be considered and in their variety, one hopefully will be of help.

FOR THOSE WHO LIKE TO "GUESSTIMATE"

1. Cut far more fabric than you think you'll need . . . use the left-overs in another project.

2. If you run out of one fabric, mix in another, match or contrast as you fancy.

3. Cut a known amount of fabric into strips, see how far it goes, use this knowledge to judge how much you still need.

4. Buy from a shop with lots more of that particular fabric . . . . just in case!

FOR THOSE WHO PREFER TO MEASURE

1. Lay a length of wool around the design cords . . . measuring this will indicate the bias length required. (Do this on 1/4 design and multiply by 4 . . . and add a little extra for luck.)

2. 1/4 yd. of 45 in. wide cotton fabric yields approximately 323 in. of 1 in. wide cut bias strip.

3. The following table shows the length of 1 in. wide bias which can be cut from fabric squares of various size.

square	bias	square	bias
8 in. =	50 in.	15 in. =	200 in.
9 in. =	72 in.	16½ in. =	242 in.
10½ in. =	98 in.	17½ in. =	288 in.
12 in. =	128 in.	19 in. =	338 in.
13½ in. =	162 in.	20½ in. =	392 in.
		22 in. =	450 in.

CUTTING BIAS STRIPS

Cutting bias from a length of fabric can leave an awkward 45° shaped point behind. This is difficult to use later. Cutting a square first, then cutting that into strips is more economic. Sometimes however you may wish to cut a full fabric width, for larger projects or using up leftovers. The following method is quick and easy.

1.

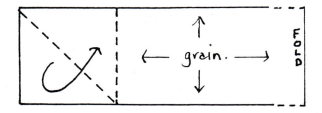

Fold fabric width in half after removing the selvedges. Flip bottom left hand corner up to find square. Check grain, if it is straight, cutting diagonally across this square will give you true bias. The further it is from straight the less stretchy your bias will be, making it harder to use. If grain is 'skewed', abandon the fabric.

2.

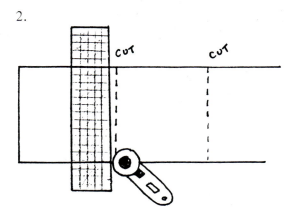

Rotary cut this square. Lay it down on the neighbouring piece of fabric and cut another square. Continue across the width of fabric. There is often an 'odd bit' remaining at the end, spread it flat on top of the fabric stack.

3.

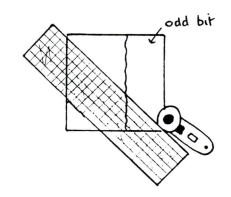

If your ruler has a 45° angle marked use it to line up a cut at this angle to the grain. If not cut corner to corner diagonally across square.

4.

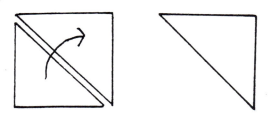

Flip the left hand triangular fabric stack over on top of the right. Line up the diagonal edge. Cutting from a 45 in. wide fabric 1/4 yd. can create up to 10 layers. It is possible to cut these all together, if you are confident and careful. If in doubt cut in batches of 4 layers at a time. If the diagonal edge is longer than your ruler fold it in half to cut.

5.

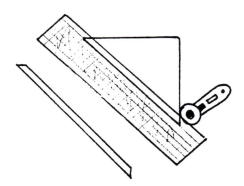

Whilst maintaining a perfectly aligned diagonal edge measure and cut strips of an appropriate width for your chosen bias bar. I would suggest . . . . 3/4 in. for 1/4 in. bar, 1 in. for 3/8 in. bar, 1.1/4 in. for 1/2 in. bar.

6.

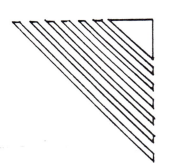

Do not cut the extremely short strips from the triangle point. Any bias length under 3 ins. is unlikely to be useful . . . . keep them for another scrap project.

SEWING BIAS INTO TUBES

All the cut strips need to be folded in half along their length and machined into tubes. A **SHORT** machine stitch is best for this purpose. These tubes will later be ironed flat so that the seam can be hidden on the underside.

IMPORTANT : Fold all strips with the right side on the outside, as they will not be turned inside out.

The distance from the folded edge of the fabric to the sewing line, must create a snug tube into which the chosen size of bias bar will fit comfortably, with no spare room. It is advisable to sew a short length of tube as a trial, to get this width exactly right.

I machine the tube with the fold on the right hand side, using a flat sided magnet stuck to the machine bed as a guide to prevent this tube width altering as I sew.

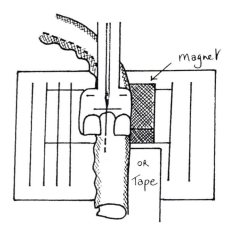

DO NOT USE MAGNETS ON COMPUTERISED MACHINES . . . . instead a short strip of masking or insulation tape correctly placed can be a useful guide, and is easily removed. If using the 1/4 in. bias bar the edge of your machine foot itself may be sufficient guide.

Bias bars tend to vary slightly in width and thickness from set to set. The three different sizes can be used as appropriate to the size of your project. My personal preference is to use 1/4 in. finished tubes which give a pleasing neat result.

Sew the strips 'factory style', feeding one after the other into the machine without a break. Overlap the pointed ends, sewing the end of one strip to the start of the next. This prevents the thin points from being 'gobbled' down into the feed dog. The colour of the thread seldom matters as it will never be seen, so it is a good job for using up oddments. This method will give you a long strip of bias tube containing unsightly joins which will be removed.

TRIMMING BIAS TUBES

1. Using a rotary cutter, cut across the tubes, eliminating all overlapped pointed ends. This will both separate the individual lengths and square off the ends. There will therefore be 2 cuts between each tube.

2. Give each tube a gentle pull to straighten it up.

3. Lay each tube down on the cutting board in turn, and carefully cut away the excess seam allowance. With a little practice and confidence this can be done to within 1/16 in. The more seam allowance trimmed away, the less bulk will lie underneath the tube when appliquéd. The short machine stitch will hold the fabric securely, preventing it splitting open during pressing.

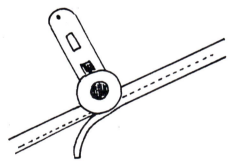

It is easier to sew, then trim away a slightly wide seam allowance, than to cut narrow fabric strips and machine them right on the cut edge. (It is probable that short lengths of either edge would be missed whilst sewing tubes, which wastes time in the tedious process of resewing the gaps.) I prefer the minimal fabric wastage and the ease of construction.

PRESSING BIAS TUBES

Having watched many quilters burn their fingers on metal bias bars, heated up by ironing on top of them (as the instructions usually direct), I felt there had to be a better way. There is!

1. Use the iron on a steam setting, or spray damp the tubes.

2. Slip the chosen bias bar inside the first fabric tube. Squash the tube along so that it all slides to the lower end of the bar.

3. Place the seam so that it runs straight, parallel to the edge of the bar, and nearer to the top than the middle so that the tube is visible on both sides of the seam allowance.

4. Holding the bar, with the seam side uppermost, slide an inch or so of tube from the lower end of the bar. Flatten it with the point of the iron in the same position as it held on the bar. Seam allowances are pressed in the same direction and not opened.

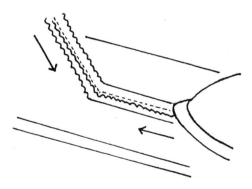

5. Keeping the iron in contact with the fabric tube, slide it towards the bar, while at the same time feeding the remaining tube off the bar towards the iron. Do not allow too much tube to slide off at once. Maintaining a short distance between iron and bar enables the seam to be pressed in the correct position throughout. Try not to stretch the tube, as it will narrow the width. Continue squashing tube down the bar, feeding it off steadily until it is completely pressed. Repeat with all tubes.

APPLIQUÉ FOR PERFECTION

If you have ever tried to anchor bias around curving designs, you will be aware of three facts . . . .

1. It frequently gathers and puckers around the inside of the curves.

2. Tacking it down on both sides to prevent puckering takes forever . . . . Pins can make it hard to handle, and they frequently fall out.

3. It is a tedious and boring task.

NOT ANY MORE!

BIAS APPLIQUÉ THE EASY WAY

The discovery of the possibility of using fusible webbing (Bondaweb™) revolutionised my Celtic Appliqué. I previously had strong reservations about bonding fabrics for appliqué since the result was stiff and flat when quilted. However in this technique so little is used in any one place, it is undetectable, and the item will quilt beautifully into soft 'hills and valleys'.

It took considerable experimentation before I could describe a problem free method. Bondaweb™ can separate from its backing paper at the least convenient moment. Once separated it becomes impossible to use for this technique. This problem has to be overcome. Here's how . . . .

BONDAWEB™ 'BUYING TIPS'

1. Buy Bondaweb™ from the roll, not in packets, taking at least 1 yd. at a time.

2. Reject battered Bondaweb™ which is already separating.

3. Insist that it is rolled and not folded.

4. Remove the coloured plastic 'ideas' sheet.

PREPARING BONDAWEB™ FOR CUTTING

1. Roll the Bondaweb™ into a loose roll, with the backing paper on the outside.

2. Place your fingers inside one end of the roll to support it, and hold it clear of any surface. LIGHTLY slide a warm, dry iron up and down over the cut edge, and the area immediately following on from it, turning the roll to facilitate this.

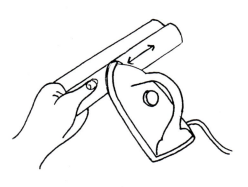

This application of gentle heat will ensure good adhesion of the webbing to the backing paper for some time, but not permanently. This heating may have to be repeated if there is a future tendency to separate.

3. Allow the Bondaweb™ to become completely cold before attempting to unroll it for cutting. (Put it in the freezer for a few minutes if you are in a big hurry!) If it is slightly sticky or hard to unroll . . . . don't . . . . it's not cold.

4. Have a close look at, and feel both sides of the Bondaweb™, so that you can easily distinguish the backing paper side once the sheet is cut. (The webbing is grainy and fibrous.)

5. Lay the roll on the cutting board with the backing paper side down. If the webbing is next to the cutting board it is inclined to adhere to any roughness and separate.

6. Using ruler and rotary cutter with a sharp blade (doubtful blades also cause separation) cut thin strips across the width of the webbing sheet. Match the width to that of your pressed tubes. I do not measure this, cutting 'by eye' is sufficient since a fraction over or under does not matter.

7. Do not cut more than three or four webbing strips at a time. Thin strips separate easily. I keep my ironing board beside a table for my cutting board, so that I can cut and apply webbing strips one at a time.

8. Apply a webbing strip to the back (seam side) of each tube, along its entire length, using a moderately hot iron. Guide the strip, paper uppermost, with one hand while the iron, held in the other sticks it on. The webbing strip should cover the back of the tube, and therefore stick to the tube itself on both sides of the seam allowance. When one strip runs out, stick another, butting the ends and leaving no gaps.

9. **DO NOT** remove the backing paper once the strip is stuck down. It identifies prepared strips which are ready to use. However it does not matter if paper comes off accidentally as it is possible to see the fused webbing if you look carefully.

10. Any webbing which sticks to the iron plate can easily be removed with a light rub of a nylon scouring pad, or prevented by ironing through paper. It is a good idea to cover the ironing board with paper or a cloth to prevent surplus webbing sticking, if it overlaps the edge of tubes.

COMPLETING THE DESIGN

Remove the backing paper from each prepared bias tube as you need it. It will now be easy to coax the tubing around the cord paths in your design. It will stick in place as you go when ironed. You will find it remains as placed, moulding around curves and loops with ease helped by the point of the iron.

1. Begin applying the bias tubing at any 'under' intersection on the transferred design. Lay the tubing along the path of a cord, ironing it as you go. The iron needs to be sufficiently hot to activate the webbing through two layers of tube fabric. (Test the temperature first on the chosen fabric if using Lurex or similar.) Follow the curves and loops until the tubing runs out always ending at an 'under' intersection for the cord you are following.

2. Turn the fabric around to enable you to point the iron in whatever direction is required with ease. There are no prizes for becoming a contortionist!

3. When you meet another bias tube already adhered, and have to pass beneath it, gently poke the tip of the bias bar under and unstick about 1/2 in. to form an 'underpass'. The 'over' tube will lift easily allowing the other to be threaded underneath and continue on its way.

4. The Embroidery pencil line will enable you to distinguish 'overs' from 'unders', but should you make a mistake there is no problem. Simply lift the wrongly positioned tube, replace it correctly and iron down. You will have 2–3 're-sticking' chances before the Bondaweb™ 'dies'. Even if this happens it is easy to adhere another webbing strip to the back and continue. However tubing which has been stretched around tight loops is better cut away and disgarded.

5. End all bias tubes as they began, half way under an intersection. Cut the 'finishing' end

to match the angle of the transfer pencil line for the cord which will cover it. Trim the 'starting' end of the new tube to butt tightly, no gaps, or overlaps. A slightly angled end will often ease the next curve.

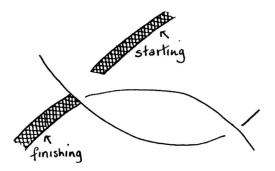

6. Keep short lengths of tubing which need to be cut off because they are not long enough to reach the next 'under' intersection enabling them to finish. They can often be incorporated on short runs elsewhere in the design.

7. Points and changes of direction in the design cords can be achieved by folding the bias tube on top of itself and ironing down, creating a mitre.

MACHINE APPLIQUÉ

This compliments the previous technique, giving a finish which if well done is both fast and of high quality. It requires, a suitable thread, correctly sized machine needle, good working light, and **PRACTICE**.

Far from being a poor second to hand appliqué, a competently machine stitched item is often mistaken for hand work. Of course the added bonus is the time saved.

The sewing machine used must have the capacity to do an automatic blind hemstitch, a variety of . . . .

_ _ _ ʌ _ _ _ʌ _ _ _ʌ _ _ _ʌ _ _ _ʌ _ _ _ʌ _

It must also have the additional possibility of reducing both the stitch length and width to a minimum. Unfortunately this latter point is not possible on all machines, even new and computerised ones. Their smallest stitch and shortest length may still be too large to compete with hand stitching. (On my Bernina I set it at between 1/2 − 1 on both settings.)

If your machine doesn't blindstitch, or cannot reduce the stitch almost to invisibility you have several possibilities.

1. Hand stitch the tubing in place.

2. Use a straight machine stitch around the tubing on both side edges.

3. Use a small zig-zag stitch around the tubing side edges.

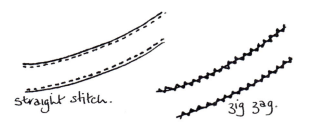

straight stitch.

zig zag.

THREAD : a soft fine transparent nylon thread is best in the machine needle, whilst a colour thread matched to the background fabric colour is in the bobbin. Contrary to popular myth, nylon thread does not melt when ironed, and is almost invisible when sewn with a short stitch. It is best obtained from specialist suppliers, in 'clear', and 'smoke' colour which is best for dark fabrics. Beware of transparent thread from other sources, it can be more suited to fishing than appliqué!

If the bobbin thread is tightened, any tendency for it to be seen on the top of the work can be lessened or eliminated. If your bobbin case has a metal 'finger' with a hole in the end, pass the thread through this after threading the bobbin to increase the tension.

Turning the bobbin case scew 1/4 turn in a clockwise direction can be another alternative. If in doubt check the machine instruction manual. The stitch quality can also be improved by loosening the top tension slightly. Try experimenting on scrap fabric before starting on the real item.

A fine machine needle, size 70 or equivalent will make smaller holes. The desired stitch should look neat, almost invisible, yet catch the edges of the tube securely at regular intervals, as would its hand stitched equivalent.

When stitching, aim for the straight stitches in the blindhem sequence to fall on the background fabric, but as near as possible to the edge of the bias tube. The intermittant zig-zag stitch should just catch the tube's edge and hold it firmly in place.

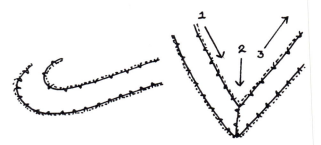

When points in the design have been mitred, the tubes folded edge also needs stitching down. Follow the sequence illustrated above . . . .

1. Approach the mitre.

2. Stitch down the fold.

3. Lift the needle and return to the edge you were stitching. Continue as before.

BE CAREFUL NOT TO MISS BITS! If you do, lift the machine foot, re-position it, go over the loose bit. It will not show.

Using a machine foot which allows clear visibility in front of the needle makes accuracy easier to achieve. (I like to use the Bernina 1/4 in. patchwork foot No. 37 which although not designed for use with swing needle stitches, still has enough clearance for this minute zig-zag to be used without breaking the needle. The foot's central straight edges help me to line up the bias tube, so that my stitches fall in exactly the right place.) A short time spent in practice at the start of each sewing session is a good 'warm-up' and improves the standard of work on finished items.

Blindhem both edges of all tubes. It makes no difference which is completed first. Whenever the way is blocked by an 'over' cord, just lift the machine foot across the cord, reposition it on the other side, leaving a thread loop which can be clipped later. If using the blindhem stitch as described there is no need to back-stitch on either side of the jumped cord. Since the stitches are set to be minute they will not come undone.

Beware . . . . as this applies also if you want to unpick them! In this instance your best hope is to snip the intermittant zig-zag, and leave the straight stitch on the backing fabric in place.

If using either straight stitch or a small zig-zag, it is necessary to anchor your stitching on both sides of the jump. Several stitches almost on top of each other will serve this purpose. (Cancel the zig-zag and run the machine for a second at fast speed while holding the fabric almost stationary against the pull of the feed dog. I call this a 'full stop'.)

Occasionally, despite the most careful checking, the odd wrongly woven intersection comes to your attention whilst you appliqué. This can be remedied by cutting through the 'over' cord and popping both ends beneath the 'under' cord . . . . changing it into an 'over' cord. This is impossible to achieve if . . . .

(a) Tube 'ends' lie under the top cord, so check this before cutting.

(b) The interlace sequence will still be wrong, even if you correct one intersection. A whole length of tube would have to be removed to correct it. Judge if it is worth the effort.

Take heart if one of the above happens. From experience I know that hardly anyone ever notices the odd mistake . . . . they can spend hours searching for it even when told it exists!

QUILTING CELTIC DESIGNS

Like all other forms of patchwork Celtic appliqué takes on an enhanced appearance when quilted. These designs can also be used solely as quilting patterns without appliqué. Quilting can of course be done by either hand or machine. 2oz. polyester wadding was used throughout the designs in this book.

The ease and speed afforded by machine quilting enables items to be elaborately textured. This is consistent with the detailed background 'filler' patterns found in Celtic manuscripts, such as the 8th Century masterpiece the 'Book of Kells'.

Quilting by machine using the same nylon thread as for appliqué gives the softest effect. This is a skill well worth developing.

WHERE TO QUILT? . . . . WHERE TO LEAVE?

There are no rules, only possibilities. You decide . . . . it is possible to alter the appearance of the same design by different quilting approaches. Some alternatives worthy of consideration are . . . .

1. **Simply Quilting** : following the double design outline exactly, creating the pattern without appliqué or colour.

2. **Contrast Quilting** : following the double design outline in a contrasting coloured thread. In addition perhaps filling the spaces between cords with machine embroidery, e.g. 'beads' of satin stitch.

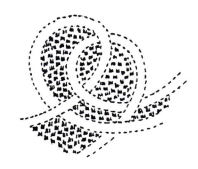

3. **Outlining** : following around both sides of the Appliquéd Cords. The best effect is obtained by doing this approximately 1/16 in. away from the edge of the bias tube. This allows the surrounded area to achieve maximum 'puff' or 'loft'.

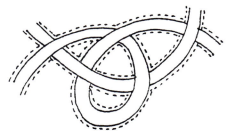

In very close complicated patterns this may cause the design to flatten, so use sparingly.

4. Selective Quilting : choosing to highlight certain shaped areas of the design, by outlining them on one side of the cord only, allowing the centre to rise.

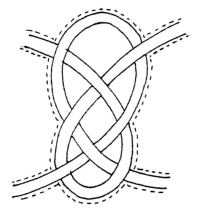

5. Contour Quilting : stitching parallel quilting lines surrounding either a whole design or certain areas. The use of a walking foot in place of the normal machine presser foot will ensure a wrinkle free finish on both the top of the quilt and on the reverse. Use the edge of the foot as a distance guide. Try altering the needle position to vary the width of the line.

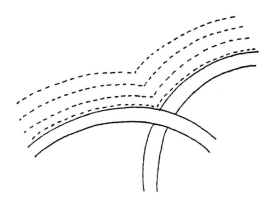

6. Free Quilting : lowering the feed-dog and fitting a machine darning foot enables you to totally control stitch length and direction. Try jig-saw puzzle shapes, spirals, key patterns etc. Great for filler designs inside shapes or around the outside of whole patterns. Control requires practice.

Tip . . . . placing a small block of wood or book beside the far side of your foot pedal, to prevent your toe depressing it further than this obstacle's thickness will aid even stitching by keeping the machine running at an even speed.

Design 4

'Rose of Tralee'

Celtic Sampler
Quilt made by
combining 12 of
16 block patterns
given.

Machine worked
throughout

(76 x 94 ins.)
Block size 16 in. square

Border detail

"Laura loves Sunsets"

Wallhanging by author, showing Celtic style border.

(44 x 54 ins.)

Design 2

Designs 7, 3 & 11

Design 8

Designs 5 & 3

Designs 13 & 10

Design 14

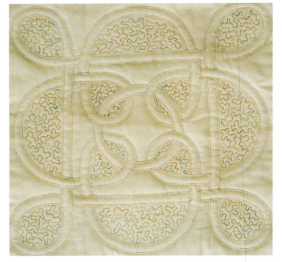

Detail of machine
embroidered cushion front

Pattern not included

Designs 7 & 1

Design 1

Details from 'Celtic Star'

'Celtic Star' Wallhanging
28 patterns . . . .
22 original (4 hand quilted
circular patterns in navy corners)
(82 x 82 ins.)

Machine embroidered cushion
satin stitch 'beads' in gold thread

detail

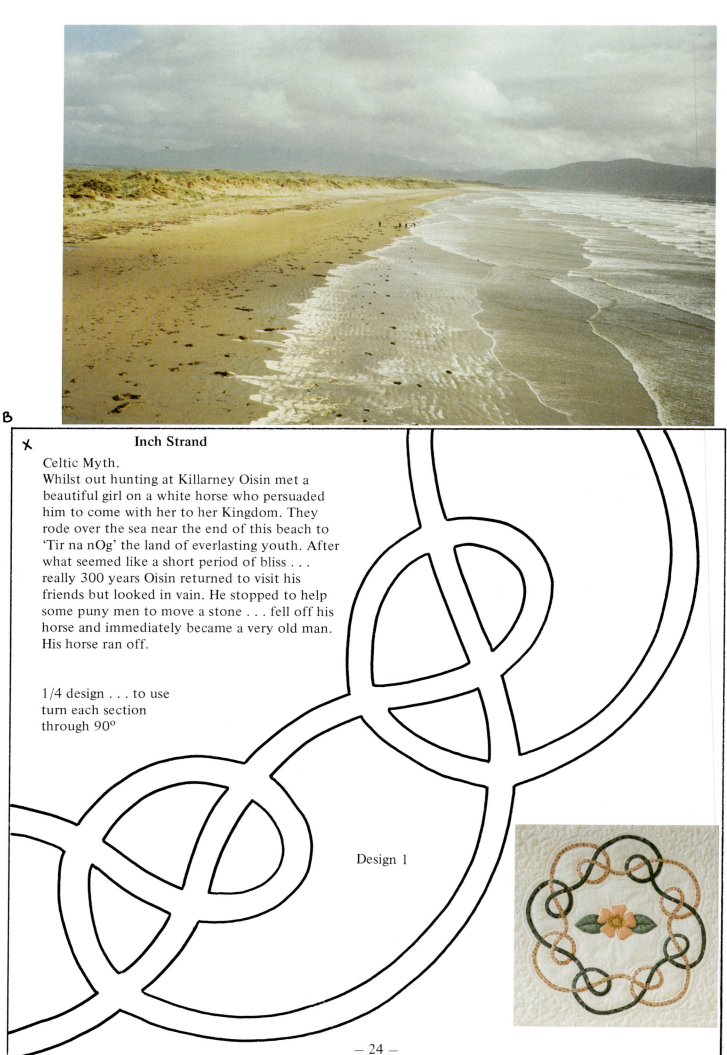

Inch Strand

Celtic Myth.
Whilst out hunting at Killarney Oisin met a beautiful girl on a white horse who persuaded him to come with her to her Kingdom. They rode over the sea near the end of this beach to 'Tir na nOg' the land of everlasting youth. After what seemed like a short period of bliss . . . really 300 years Oisin returned to visit his friends but looked in vain. He stopped to help some puny men to move a stone . . . fell off his horse and immediately became a very old man. His horse ran off.

1/4 design . . . to use
turn each section
through 90°

Design 1

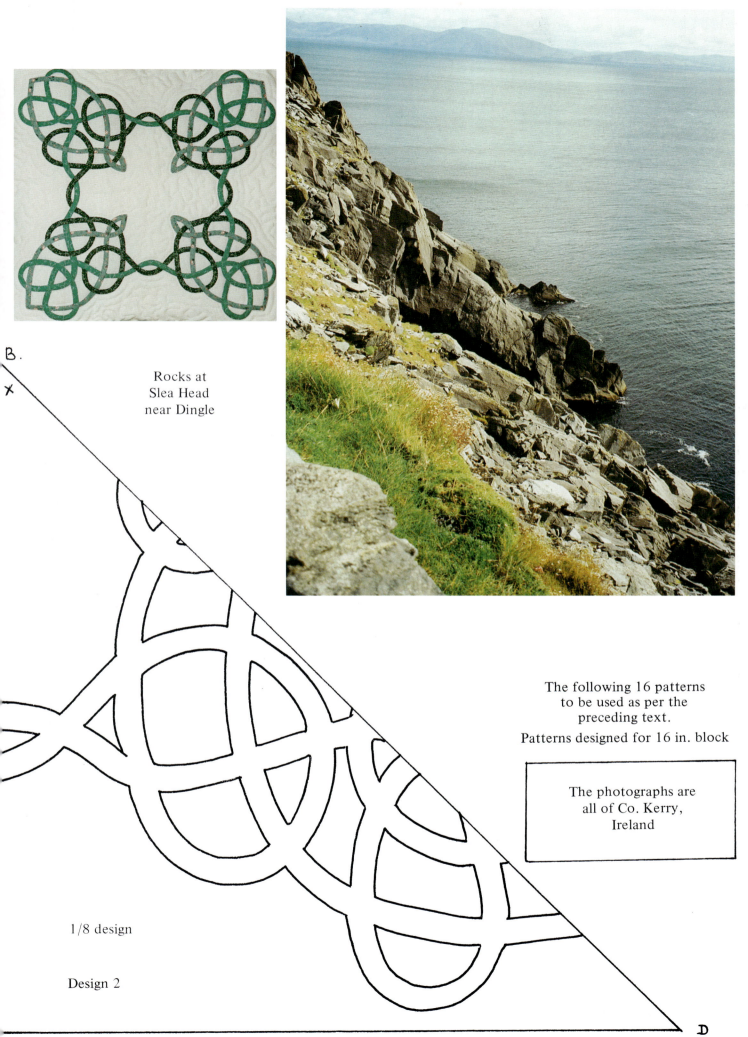

Rocks at
Slea Head
near Dingle

B.

X

D

The following 16 patterns
to be used as per the
preceding text.

Patterns designed for 16 in. block

The photographs are
all of Co. Kerry,
Ireland

1/8 design

Design 2

Wild bogland

B

X

1/8 design

A D

Design 3

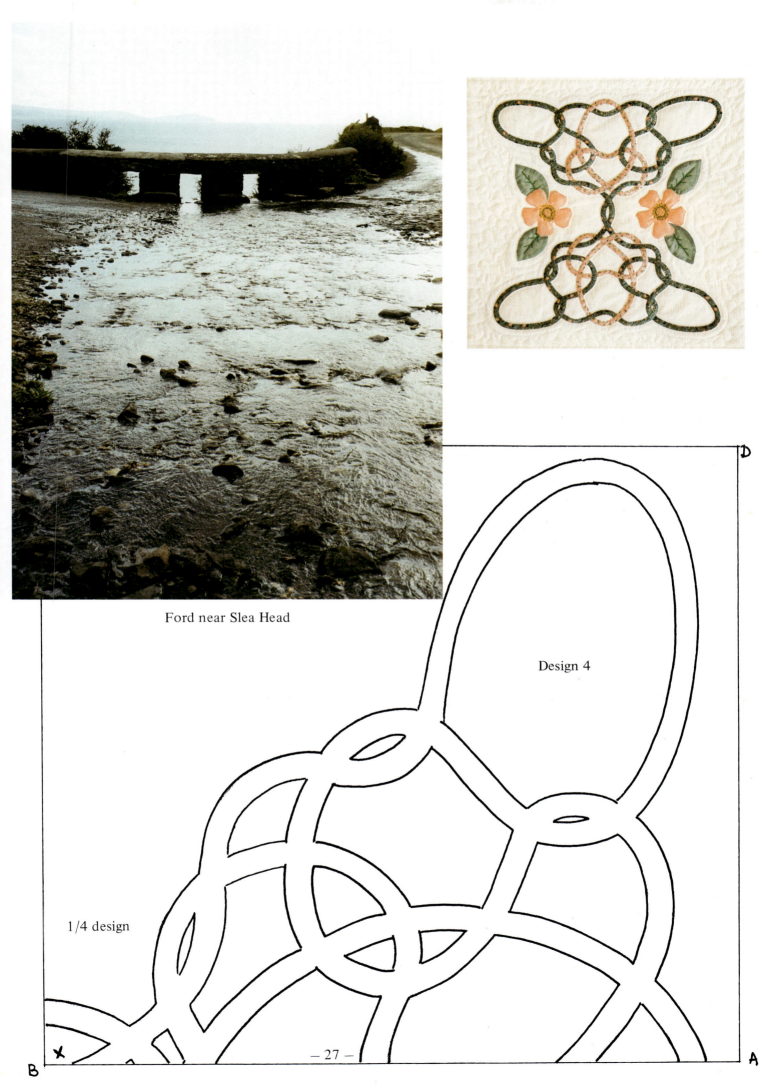

Ford near Slea Head

Design 4

1/4 design

B   X

A

D

B

X

'The Sleeping Giant'
Blasket Islands

C

Design 5

A

D

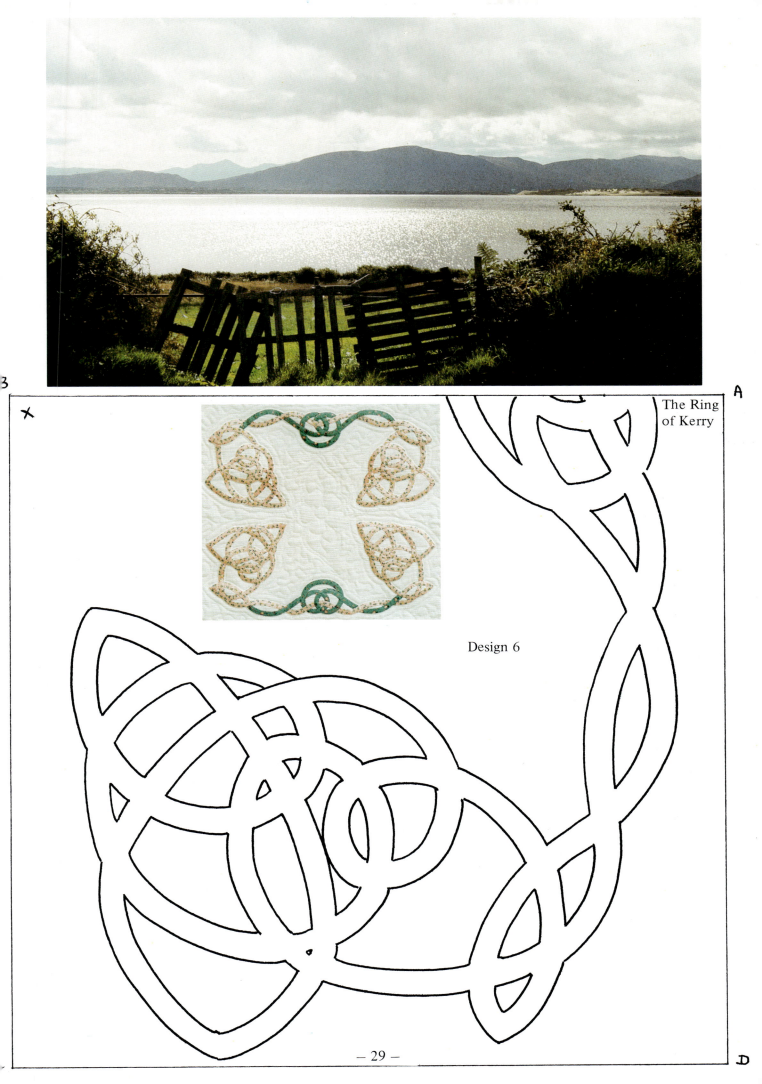

The Ring
of Kerry

Design 6

The Celts burned bracken and
briars to make soap from
the ash

Design 7

B

X

A

1/8 design

'Caherconree', the famous hill top Celtic fort, built by Cu Roi Mac Daire, magical King of Munster. (This fort became impregnable after sunset when it began to revolve with terrifying swiftness.)

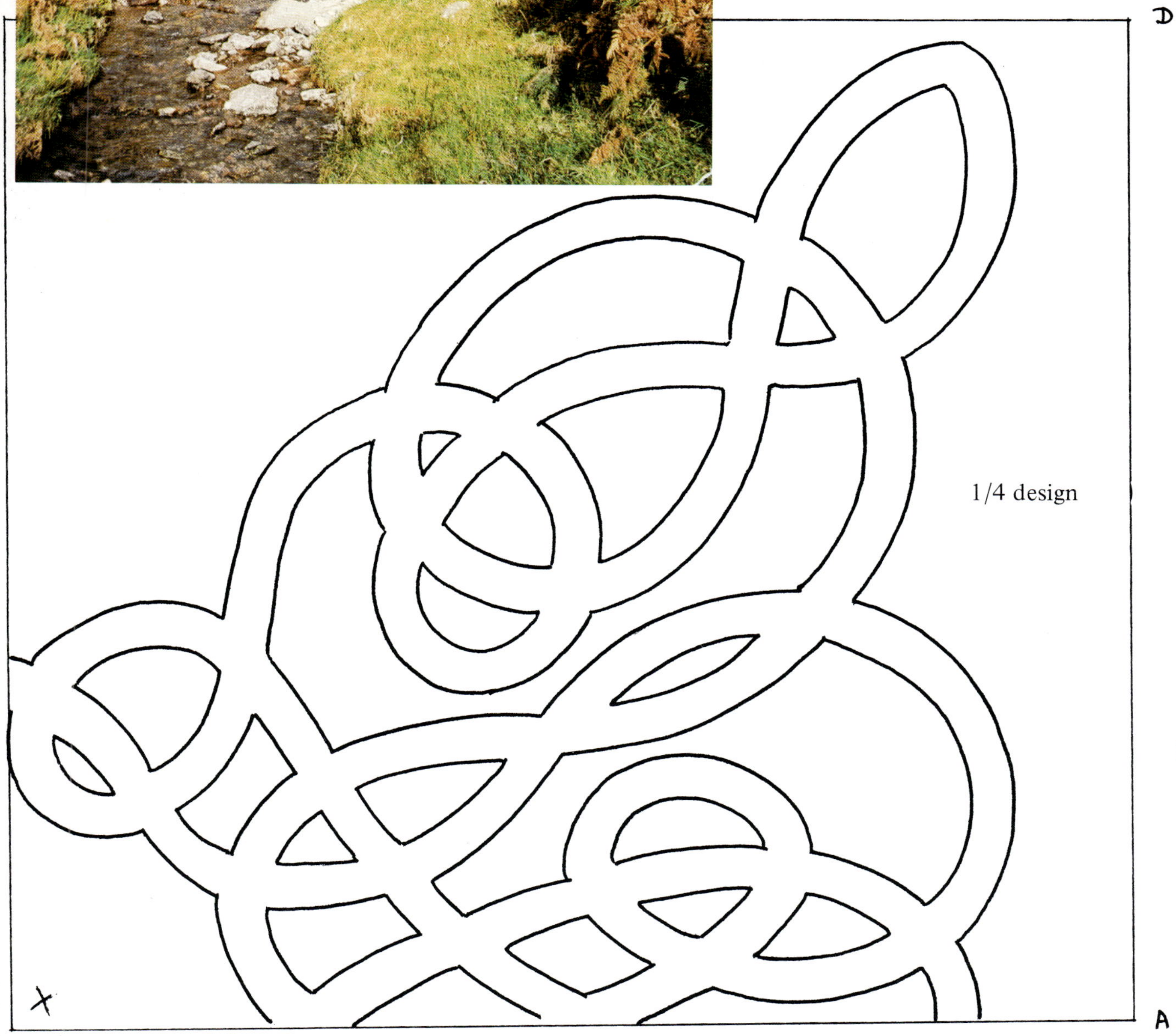

D

1/4 design

Design 8

X

A

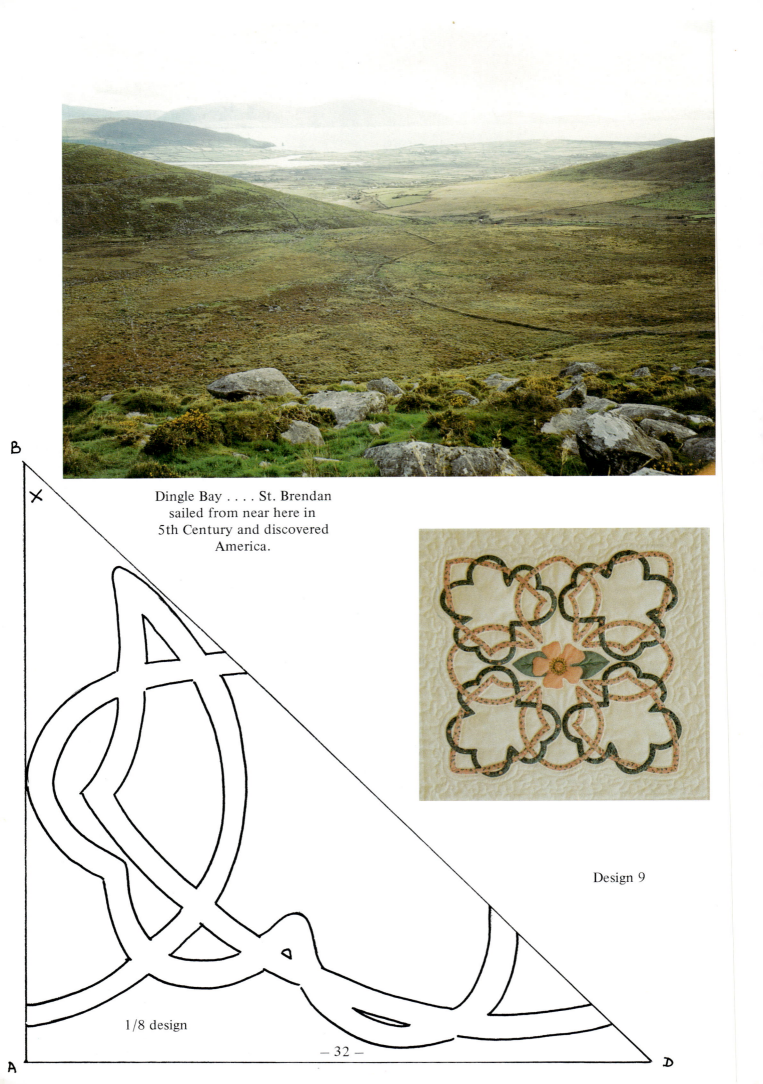

Dingle Bay . . . . St. Brendan
sailed from near here in
5th Century and discovered
America.

Design 9

B

X

A

D

1/8 design

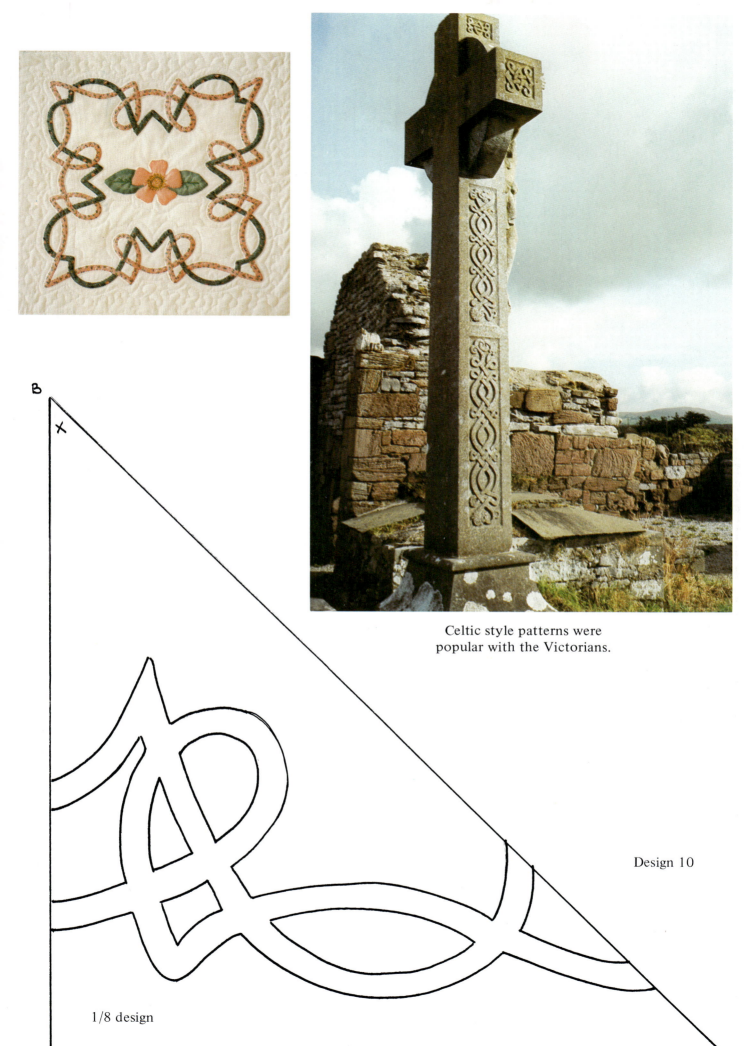

Celtic style patterns were
popular with the Victorians.

Design 10

1/8 design

B

X

A

D

Celtic crosses first appeared in
Scotland and Ireland around
7th Century A.D.

B

X

Design 11

1/8 design

A

D

The Connor Pass
The Celts maintained their roads
for 'travel, horseracing and war'.

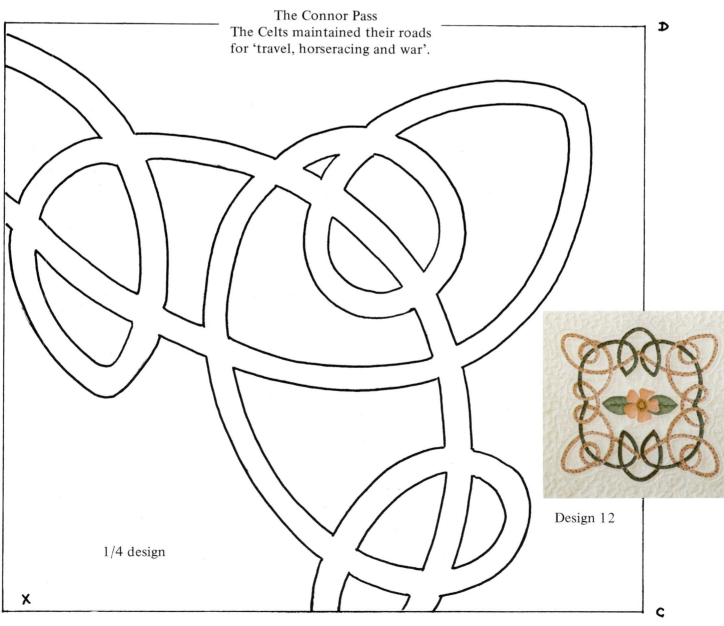

D

1/4 design

Design 12

X

C

B   ✗   Dunquin   A

Design 13

1/4 design

C   D

Dingle
Bay

B

X

C

Design 14

1/4 design

— 37 —

D

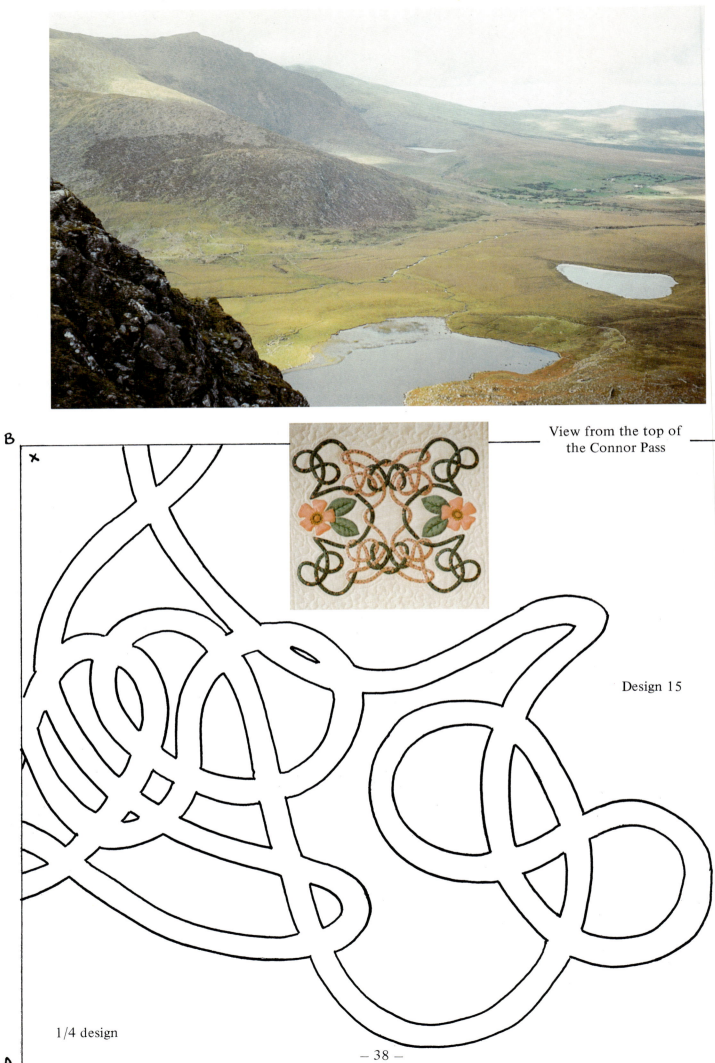

B

x

View from the top of
the Connor Pass

Design 15

1/4 design

A

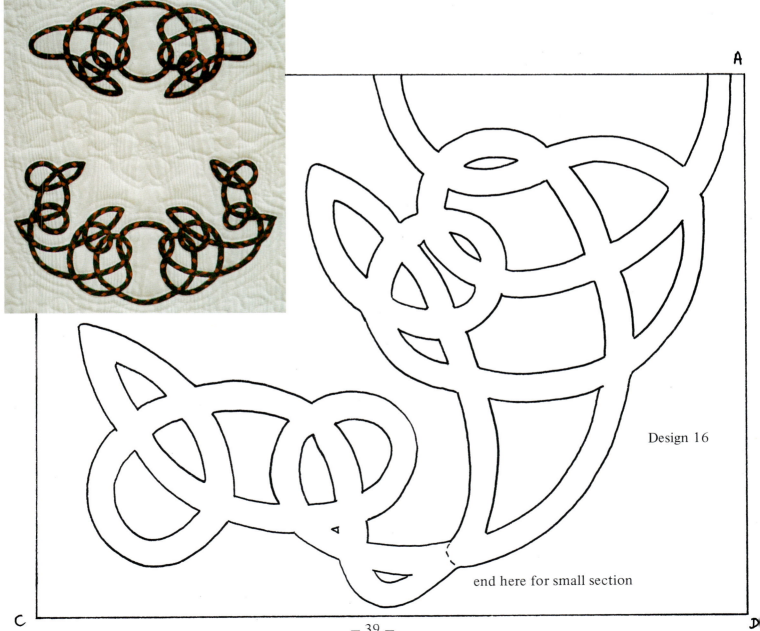

A

Design 16

end here for small section

C

D

Flower centre is machine
embroidery .... small 'beads'
of satin stitch

Optional rose
Quilting outline

Underlap
leaf

Underlap
leaf

Appliqué pattern
Optional rose
and leaves.

Seam allowance
NOT included

Leaf veins
machine quilted

Quilting twist pattern ....
Cut 2 in thin card .... can be overlapped varying amounts
in opposite directions to lengthen twist as required.

QUILTING EQUIPMENT AND FABRIC SUPPLIERS

QUILT BASICS
2 Meades Lane
Chesham
Bucks. HP5 1ND
Tel: 0494 785202

CRIMPLE CRAFT
1 Freeman's Way,
Forest Lane,
Weatherby Road
Harrogate HG3 1RW
Tel: 0423 885430

'CHATTELS'
53 Chalk Farm Road
London
NW1 8AN
Tel: 071 267 0877

COTTON PATCH
1285 Stratford Road
Hall Green
Birmingham B28
Tel: 021 702 2804

VILLAGE FABRICS
Unit 7, Bushells Business Estate
Wallingford
Oxfordshire OX10 9DD
Tel: 0491 36178

QUILTERS PLACE LTD
17 North Methven Street
Perth
Scotland
Tel: 0738 30128

THE VOIRREY
EMBROIDERY CENTRE
Brimstage Hall
Wirral L63 6JA
Tel: 051 342 3514

THE QUILT ROOM
20 West Street
Dorking
Surrey RH4 1BL
Tel: 0306 740739

QUILT ART ACCESSORIES
The Hill House, Tipper Road
Naas, Co. Kildare
Ireland
Tel: 045 76121

BIBLIOGRAPHY

DAVIS, COURTNEY . . . . *'Celtic Borders and Decoration'* . . . . BLANDFORD 1992

BAIN, IAIN . . . . *'Celtic Knotwork'* . . . . CONSTABLE 1986

BAIN, GEORGE . . . . *Celtic Art, the Methods of Construction* . . . . CONSTABLE 1951

HARGRAVE, HARRIET . . . . . *Mastering Machine Appliqué* . . . . C. T. PUBLISHING 1991

LAING, LLOYD . . . . *Later Celtic Art* . . . . SHIRE ARCHAEOLOGY 1987

MEGAW, RUTH & VINCENT . . *Early Celtic Art* . . . . SHIRE ARCHAEOLOGY 1986

MEGAW, RUTH & VINCENT . . *'Celtic Art from its beginnings to the Book of Kells'* . . . . THAMES AND HUDSON 1989

WIECHEC, PHILOMENA . . . . . *Celtic Quilt Designs* . . . . CELTIC DESIGN CO. 1980

NOTES